Spy It!

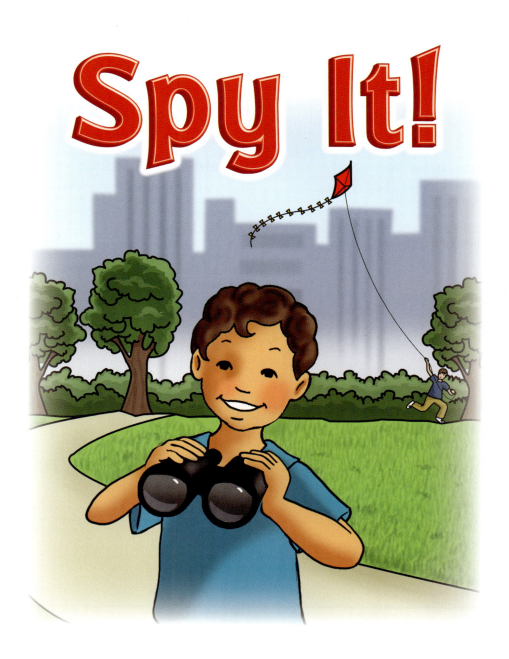

Suzanne I. Barchers

Consultants

Robert C. Calfee, Ph.D.
Stanford University

P. David Pearson, Ph.D.
University of California, Berkeley

Publishing Credits

Dona Herweck Rice, *Editor-in-Chief*
Lee Aucoin, *Creative Director*
Sharon Coan, M.S.Ed., *Project Manager*
Jamey Acosta, *Editor*
Robin Erickson, *Designer*
Cathie Lowmiller, *Illustrator*
Robin Demougeot, *Associate Art Director*
Heather Marr, *Copy Editor*
Rachelle Cracchiolo, M.S.Ed., *Publisher*

Teacher Created Materials

5301 Oceanus Drive
Huntington Beach, CA 92649-1030
http://www.tcmpub.com

ISBN 978-1-4333-2910-4

© 2012 by Teacher Created Materials, Inc.
Printed in China
Nordica.062019.CA21900606

Mike can spy things.
Try it!

Mike can spy the pile.
Can you spy the file?

Mike can spy the lime.
Can you spy the dime?

Mike can spy the bike.
Can you spy the trike?

Mike can spy the hive.
Can you spy the five?

Mike can spy the fries.
Can you spy the flies?

Mike can spy the pie.
Can you spy the tie?

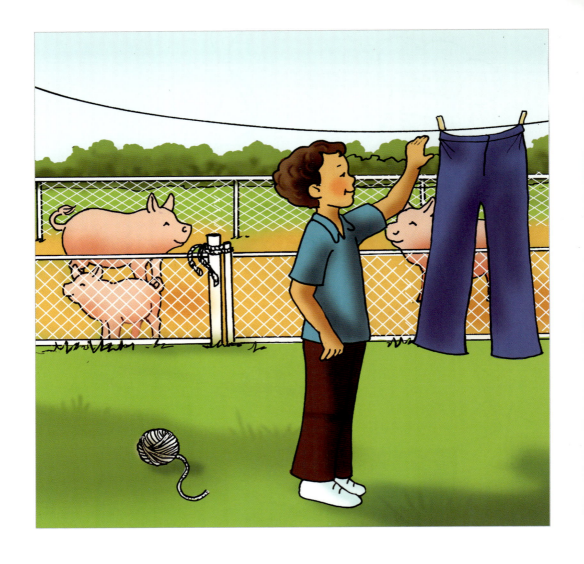

Mike can spy the line. Can you spy the twine?

Mike can spy the bride. Can you spy the slide?

Mike can spy the rice.
Can you spy the mice?

Mike can spy the slice.
Can you spy the spice?

What can you spy that has a long *i*?

Decodable Words

bike	hive	rice
bride	it	slice
can	lime	slide
dime	line	spice
file	long	spy
five	mice	tie
flies	Mike	trike
fries	pie	try
has	pile	twine

Sight Words

a	things
that	what
the	you

Extension Activities

Discussion Questions

- What are some of the things that Mike spied? (*bike*, *bride*, *fries*, *hive*, *lime*, *line*, *pie*, *pile*, *rice*, and *slice*)
- What were you asked to spy? (*dime*, *file*, *five*, *flies*, *mice*, *slide*, *spice*, *tie*, *trike*, and *twine*)
- Look at page 14. What can you spy that has the long *i* sound? (*bike*, *bride*, *ice cream*, *kite*, *mice*, *ride*, *sky*, *slide*, *smile*, *trike*, *twine*)

Exploring the Story

- Write the word *Mike* on a sheet of paper. Make a list of the words that rhyme with *Mike*, such as *bike*, *hike*, *Ike*, *like*, *pike*, *spike*, and *trike*. Which words begin with a blend of two consonants? (*spike and trike*.)
- Play the game "I Spy." The first player secretly chooses something that can be seen, says "I spy with my little eye a ___ ," and gives one clue about the item. The other players take turns guessing the item. With each incorrect guess, the first player provides an additional clue. The guessing continues until the item is identified. The person who guesses correctly takes the next turn.
- When on a walk or in a vehicle, try to spy things that have the long *i* sound. Take time to review other vowel sounds, such as long *a*.